KU-678-713

TELL ME
ABOUT

2/98

Evans

Evans Brothers Limited

Published by Evans Brothers Limited
2A Portman Mansions
Chiltern Street
London W1M 1LE

© Evans Brothers Limited 1997

First published 1997

Printed by Graficas Reunidas SA, Spain

British Library Cataloguing in Publication data.

Malam, John
 Tell me about Roger Hargreaves
 1. Hargreaves, Roger, 1935-1988 – Criticism and interpretation –
Juvenile literature 2. Novelists, English – 20th century –
Biography – Juvenile literature
 I. Title II.Roger Hargreaves
 823 .9'14

ISBN 0237517582

Roger Hargreaves wrote books for children. One day, while he was at work, he drew a picture of a little character with very long arms. He called him Mr Tickle. Later, he wrote a story to go with the picture. This was how the Mr Men and Little Miss characters began. Roger Hargreaves wrote more than seventy Mr Men and Little Miss books. This is his story.

Roger Hargreaves, who created the famous Mr Men and Little Miss characters

Roger Hargreaves was born on the 9th of May, 1935. He was born in Cleckheaton, a small town in west Yorkshire. His parents were Reginald and Ethel Hargreaves. Roger's father owned a laundry and dry-cleaning business. Roger had two brothers and a sister. He was the second oldest.

Roger with his parents and younger brother and sister

Cleckheaton, where Roger was born

From an early age, Roger showed a liking for art. He liked to draw cartoons. He was once asked about this and he said: "When I was fifteen or sixteen I wanted to be a cartoonist. I thought it would be a wonderful life because you could live anywhere you liked and work at any time."

Roger with his little brother, Richard

Roger went to Sowerby Bridge Grammar School.

7

Like many boys his age, Roger loved sport, especially cricket. He supported Yorkshire County Cricket Club, and sometimes he went to watch the team play.

When Roger left school he went to work in his father's laundry and dry-cleaning business.

Roger and his family often went on holiday to the Yorkshire coast.

The Hargreaves family and friends on holiday in Scarborough. Roger is between his mother and older brother Robert.

One day an important letter arrived at Roger's house. It was from the government. It told him he had to do National Service. This meant he had to join the army, the navy or the air force for two years. Roger chose the Royal Air Force. The year was 1955. Roger was twenty years old.

Young men in Britain used to do National Service. It was a way of training them to be soldiers in case there was a war.

Young men starting their National Service in the 1950s.

When Roger left National Service, he found a job as a copywriter in an advertising company in Bradford. He learned that the best adverts have very few words and good, clear pictures.

After two years Roger moved to London. In London he wrote lots of different adverts. He wrote adverts that helped to sell cars, petrol, spaghetti, chocolate and watches. It was exciting work, and he went on trips all over the world.

Roger in Paris

10

Roger and Christine on their wedding day

Roger married Christine in 1960. They had four children. Roger wanted to spend more time at home with his family. So he had to find a different job. He wondered if he could write books for children, and draw funny pictures to go with his stories. He could do this at home.

He said: "They have to be small books because small children like small books, and they have to be funny with a picture on every page."

In 1971, when Roger was thirty-six years old, he had an idea. He said: "Who knows what a tickle looks like?" No one could tell him, so he drew what he thought one should look like. He said: "A tickle is small and round and has arms that stretch and stretch and stretch."

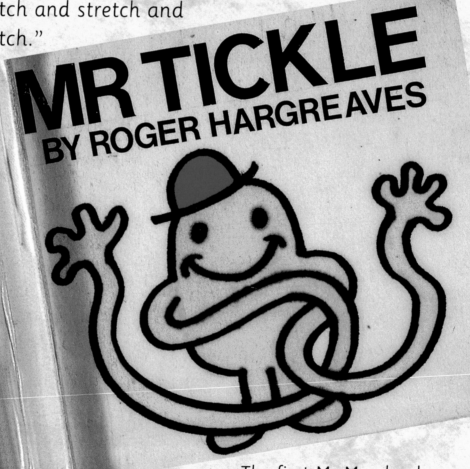

The first Mr Men book ever, which Roger made by hand

Roger called his character Mr Tickle. He wrote a funny story about how Mr Tickle tickled a teacher, a policeman, a doctor and a postman. He made lots of colourful pictures to go with the story.

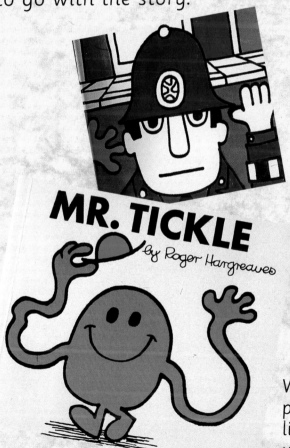

When Mr Tickle was printed, the book looked like this. Can you guess who all the characters are?

Mr Tickle

Roger drew some other characters and wrote funny stories about them.
He soon had six little books. They were Mr Tickle, Mr Greedy, Mr Happy, Mr Nosey, Mr Sneeze and Mr Bump. The books were called the Mr Men books. People liked them and they started to ask for more stories. Soon, Roger was able to work from home all the time, writing and drawing new Mr Men books.

Mr Greedy

Mr Happy

Mr Nosey

Mr Sneeze

Mr Bump

Roger wrote forty-three different Mr Men books. His favourite was Mr Silly because he liked his silly sense of humour.

Mr Silly

Roger reads a bedtime story to his children, Sophie, Amelia, Adam and Giles.

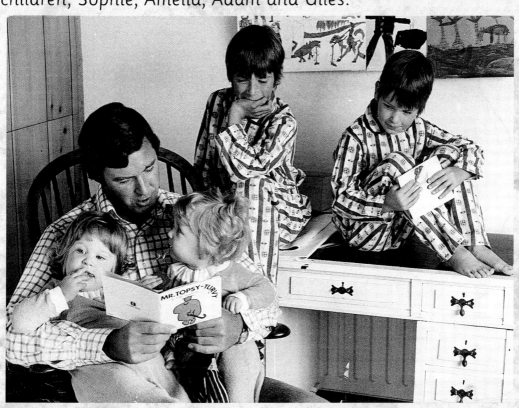

In 1979, Roger and his family went to live on the island of Guernsey. Guernsey is one of the Channel Islands. Roger had always wanted to live on an island.

On Guernsey, Roger lived in an old house in the middle of the island.

One wall of his study was filled with shelves full of Mr Men books and toys. On his desk were the Mr Men drawings he was always working on.

Guernsey, where Roger lived for three years

16

Roger used felt pens to draw the pictures in all his Mr Men books. He said: "I often leave the smile until the next day. I love to come down in the morning and fill it in. It's the smile that brings them alive."

Mr Happy

Roger in his study, at work on a new picture

Ten years after the first Mr Men books appeared, Roger was asked to write some new books. They were called Little Miss books. There was Little Miss Bossy, Little Miss Neat, Little Miss Sunshine, and all their friends. Roger's favourite was Little Miss Chatterbox.

About four million Mr Men and Little Miss books are sold in Britain every year. Roger wrote lots of other books for children too. He even wrote a book called "I Am A Book". It was a rhyme book about how it might feel to be a pencil, the ocean or even a sausage!

They have been translated into more than fifteen different languages and are loved by children all over the world.

Mr Nosey in Welsh

Mr Funny in Japanese

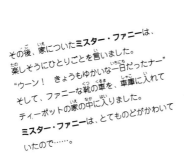

その後、家についた**ミスター・ファニー**は、
楽しそうにひとりごとを言いました。
"ウーン！ きょうもゆかいな一日だったナー"
そして、ファニーな靴の車を、車庫に入れて
ティーポットの家の中に入りました。
ミスター・ファニーは、とてものどがかわいて
いたので……。

Roger signs his autograph for some of his fans.

Roger Hargreaves died in 1988. He was fifty-three years old.

The Mr Men and Little Miss characters that Roger created have starred in their own television series, and they have appeared on everything from birthday cards to wallpaper.

Roger once said: "I feel very happy to think that when the Mr Men and Little Misses are 100 years old, their readers will always be five."

Important dates

1935	Roger Hargreaves was born in Cleckheaton, Yorkshire
1940	He went to primary school at Goole, Yorkshire
1947	He went to Sowerby Bridge Grammar School, Sowerby Bridge, Yorkshire
1953	He began to work in his father's laundry and dry-cleaning business
1955	He joined the Royal Air Force and did two years' National Service in London
1958	He moved back to Yorkshire and joined an advertising company in Bradford
1959	He moved to London to work for advertising companies
1960	Roger married Christine
1971	The first Mr Men books were published
1975	The Mr Men were first seen on television
1979	He went to live on Guernsey, in the Channel Islands
1981	The first Little Miss books were published
1982	He moved back to England
1988	Roger Hargreaves died

Keywords

advertisement (advert)
a notice or a short film about a product that is for sale

Channel Islands
a group of islands in the English Channel, 10km (6 miles) from France

cartoonist
someone who draws cartoon pictures

copywriter
someone who writes the words for adverts

Index